by John Berryman

POEMS   1942

THE DISPOSSESSED   1948

HOMAGE TO MISTRESS BRADSTREET   1956

77 DREAM SONGS   1964

HIS TOY, HIS DREAM, HIS REST   1968

SHORT POEMS   1967

BERRYMAN'S SONNETS   1967

THE DREAM SONGS   1969

LOVE & FAME   1970

DELUSIONS, ETC.   1972

DELUSIONS, ETC.

of

JOHN BERRYMAN

 NEW YORK

FARRAR, STRAUS AND GIROUX

FIRST EDITION, 1972

Printed in the United States of America
Published simultaneously in Canada
by Doubleday Canada Ltd., Toronto

Acknowledgments are made to the editors of *The
New Yorker*, in which "Ecce Homo" and "King David
Dances" were first published; and for other poems
to the editors of *Esquire*, *The Harvard Advocate*,
and *The New York Review*.

We haue piped vnto you, and ye haue not danced:
wee haue mourned vnto you, and ye haue not lamented.

*On parle toujours de 'l'art réligieux'. L'art est
réligieux.*

And indeed if Eugène Irténev was mentally deranged
everyone is in the same case; the most mentally de-
ranged people are certainly those who see in others
indications of insanity they do not notice in themselves.

Feu! feu! feu!

Than longen folk to goon on pilgrimages

Contents

I OPUS DEI

(a layman's winter mockup, wherein moreover
the Offices are not within one day said
but thro' their hours at intervals
over many weeks—such being the World)

*Lord, have mercy on my son: for he is lunatick,
and sore vexed: for ofttimes he falleth into
the fire, and oft into the water.*

*And he did evil, because he prepared not
his heart to seek the Lord.*

Lauds

LET us rejoice on our cots, for His nocturnal miracles
antique outside the Local Group & within it
& within our hearts in it, and for quotidian miracles
parsees-off yielding to the Hale reflector.

Oh He is potent in the corners. Men
with Him are potent: quasars we intuit,
and sequent to sufficient discipline
we perceive this glow keeping His winter out.

My marvellous black new brim-rolled felt is both stuffy & raffish.
I hit my summit with it, in firelight.
Maybe I only got a Yuletide tie
(increasing sixty) & some writing-paper

but ha (ha*ha*) I've bought myself a hat!
Plus-strokes from position zero! Its feathers sprout.
Thank you, Your Benevolence!
permissive, smiling on   our silliness You forged.

Matins

Thou hard. I will be blunt: Like widening
blossoms again glad toward Your soothe of sun
& solar drawing forth, I find meself
little this bitter morning, Lord, tonight.

Less were you tranquil to me in my dark
just now than tyrannous. O some bore down
sore with enticements—One abandoned me—
half I swelled up toward—till I crash awake.

However, lo, across what wilderness
in vincible ignorance past forty years
lost to (as now I see) Your sorrowing
I strayed abhorrent, blazing with my Self.

I thought I was in private with the Devil
hounding me upon Daddy's cowardice
(trustless in stir the freeze: 'Do your own time').
Intertangled all—choking, groping bodies.

'Behold, thou art taken in thy mischief,
because thou art a bloody man' with horror
loud down from Heaven did I not then hear,
but sudden' was received,—appointed even

poor scotographer, far here from Court,
humming over goodnatured Handel's Te Deum.
I waxed, upon surrender, strenuous
ah almost able service to devise.

I am like your sun, Dear, in a state of shear—
parts of my surface are continually slipping past others,
not You, not You. O I may, even, wave
in crisis like a skew Wolf-Rayet star.

Seas and hills, the high lakes, Superior,
accomplish your blue or emerald donations—
manifest too your soft forbearance, hard
& flint for fierce man hardly to take in.

I take that in. Yes. Just now. I read that.

Hop foot to foot, hurl the white pillows about,
jubilant brothers: He is our overlord,
holding up yet with crimson flags the Sun
whom He'll embark soon mounting fluent day!

Prime

OCCLUDES wild dawn. Up thro' green ragged clouds
one sun is tearing, beset alders sway
weary under swollen sudden drops
and February winds shudder our doors,

Lord, as thou knowest. What fits me today
which work I can? I've to poor minimum
pared my commitments; still I'm sure to err
grievous & frequent before Evensong

and both I long toward & abhor that coming.
Yet *if* You and I make a majority
(as old Claudel encouraged) what sharp law
can pass this morning?—upon which, I take heart.

Also: 'The specific gravity of iron
is one and one-half times the size of Switzerland.'
Zany enlivens. People, pipe with pipes:
the least of us is back on contract, even

unto myself succeeding in sunrise
all over again!
                        All customary blessings,
anathemas of the date (post-Lupercal,
and sure The Baby was my valentine),

I'm not Your beaver, here disabled, still
it is an honour, where some have achieved,

to limp behind along, humming, & keen
again upon what blue trumps, hazy, vainless glory.

In Alexandria, O Saint Julian
gouty, chair-borne, displayed then on a camel
thorough the insufferable city, and burned.
In other places, many other holy

bishops, confessors, and martyrs. Thanks be to God.

Interstitial Office

Bᴉᴛᴛᴇʀ upon conviction
(even of the seven women jurors
several wept) I will not kneel just now,
Father. I know I must

but being black & galled for these young men,
sick with their savage Judge
('we felt we had no alternative,
since all their evidence was ordered stricken')—

deep fatigue.
Conducting his own defence: 'men do pass laws
that usurp God's power . . .
I hope you'll try in your own way to speak peace.

God guide you.' Grim the prosecutor:
'He's trying to weasel his way out of it.'
Draft records here would have gone up in fire.
Peasant ladies & poupies there   went up go up in fire.

Who sat thro' all three trials tells me the juror in blue
looked inconsolably sad, and hid her eyes,
when one propped up on his table a little hand-lettered sign
ᴡᴇ ʟᴏᴠᴇ ʏᴏᴜ.

The judge is called P N.
This is of record. Where slept then Your lightning?
Loafed Your torque.
Well. Help us all! Yes—yes—I kneel.

Tierce

Oн half as fearful for the yawning day
where full the Enemy's paratus and
I clearly may
wholly from prime time fail, as yet from yesterday

with good heart grateful having gone no more
(under what gentle tempting You knew I bore)
than what occurred astray,
I almost at a loss now genuflect and pray:

Twice, thrice each day five weeks at 'as we forgive
those who trespass against us' I have thought
ah his envenomed & most insolent missive
and I have *done* it!—and I damn him still

odd times & unawares catch myself at it:
I'm not a good man, I won't ever be,
there's no health in here. You expect too much.
This pseudo-monk is all but at despair.

My blustering & whining & *ill* will
versus His will—Forgive my insolence,
since when I was a fervent child to You
and Father Boniface each 5 a.m.

But this world that was not. Lavender & oval,
lilac, dissolve into one's saying hurriedly
'In sex my husband is brutal, beating, dirty, and drunk.'
Has this become Thy will, Thou Reconciler?

Sext

High noon has me pitchblack, so in hope out,
slipping thro' stasis, my heart skeps a beat
actuellement,
reflecting on the subtler menace of decline.

Who mentioned in his middle age 'Great Death
wars in us living which will have us all'
caused choreographers to tinker maps
pointing a new domestic capital

and put before Self-Preservation '1)'.
We do not know, deep now the dire age on,
if it's so, or mere a nightmare of one dark one,
Mani's by no means ultimate disciple.

I wish You would clear this up. Moreover, I know
it may extend millennia, or ever, till
you tell somebody to. Meantime: Okay.
Now hear this programme for   my remnant of today.

Corpuscle-Donor, to the dizzy tune
of half a hundred thousand while I blink
losing that horrid same
scarlet amount and reel intact ahead:

so of rare Heart repair my fracturing heart
obedient to disobedience
minutely, wholesale, that come midnight neither
my mortal sin nor thought upon it lose me.

Nones

PROBLEM. I cannot come among Your saints,
it's not in me—'Velle' eh?—I will, and fail.
But I would rather not be lost from You—
if I could hear of a middle ground, I'd opt:

a decent if minute salvation, sort of, on some fringe.
I am afraid, afraid. Brothers, who if
you are afraid are my brothers—veterans of fear—
pray with me now in the hour of our living.

It's Eleseus' grave makes the demons tremble,
I forget under what judge he conquered the world,
we're not alone here. Hearing Mark viii, though,
I'm sure to be ashamed of by. I am ashamed.

Riotous doubt assailed me on the stair,
I paused numb. Not much troubled with doubt,
not used to it. In a twinkling can man be lost?
Deep then in thought, and thought brought no relief.

But praying after, and somewhat after prayer
on no occasion fear had gone away!
I was alone with You again: 'the iron did swim'.
It has been proved to me again & again

He does *not* want me to be lost. Who does? The other.
But 'a man's shaliach is as it were himself':
I am Your person.

I have done this & that which I should do,
and given, and attended, and been still,
but why I do so I cannot be sure,
I am suspicious of myself. Help me!

I am olding & ignorant, and the work is great,
daylight is long, will ever I be done,
for the work is not for man, but the Lord God.
Now I have prepared with all my might for it

and mine O shrinks a micro-micro-minor
post-ministry, and of Thine own to Thee I have given,
and there is none abiding but woe or Heaven,
teste the pundits. Me I'm grounded for peace.

Flimsy between cloth, what may I attain
who slither in my garments? there's not enough of me,
Master, for virtue. I'm loose, at a loss.

Lo, where in this whirlpool sheltered in bone,
only less whirlpool bone, envisaging,
a sixtieth of an ounce to every pint,
sugar to blood, or coma or convulsion,

I hit a hundred and twenty notes a second
as many as I may to the glory of confronting—
unstable man, man torn by blast & gale—
Your figure, adamantly frontal.

Vespers

Vanity! hog-vanity, ape-lust
slimed half my blue day, interspersed
solely almost with conversation feared,
difficult, dear, leaned forward toward & savoured,

survivaling between. I have not done well.
Contempt—if even the man be judged sincere—
verging on horror, top a proper portion,
of the poor man in paracme, greeding still.

That's nothing, nothing! For his great commands
have reached me here—to love my enemy
as I love me—which is quite out of the question!
and worse still, to love You *with my whole mind*—

insufferable & creative addition to Deuteronomy 6—

Shift! Shift!
   Frantic I cast about abroad
for avenues of out: Who really this this?
Can *all* be lost, then? (But some do these things . . .
I flinch from some horrible saints half the happy mornings—

so that's blocked off.) Maybe it's *not* God's voice
only Christ's only. (But our Lord is our Lord.
No vent there.) If more's demanded of man than can
man summon, You're unjust. Suppose not. See Jewish history,

tormented & redeemed, millennia later
in Freud & Einstein forcing us sorry & free,
Jerusalem Israeli! flames Anne Frank
a beacon to the Gentiles weltering.

With so great power bitter, so marvellous mild even mercy?
It's not conformable. It must be so,
but I am lost in it, dire Friend. Only I remember
of Solomon's cherubim 'their faces were inward'.

And thro' that veil of blue, & crimson, & linen,
& blue, You brood across forgiveness and
the house fills with a cloud, so that the priests
cannot stand to minister   by reason of the cloud.

Compline

I WOULD at this late hour as little as may be
(in-negligent Father) plead. Not that I'm not attending,
only I kneel here spelled
under a mystery of one midnight

un-numbing now toward sorting in & out
I've got to get as little as possible wrong
O like Josiah then I heard with horror
instructions ancient as for the prime time

I am the king's son who squat down in rags
declared unfit by wise friends to inherit
and nothing of me left but skull & feet
& bloody among their dogs the palms of my hands.

Adorns my crossbar Your high frenzied Son,
mute over catcalls. How to conduct myself?
Does 'l'affabilité, l'humilité'
drift hither from the Jesuit wilderness,

a programme so ambitious? I am ambitious
but I have always stood content with towers
& traffic quashing thro' my canyons wild,
gunfire & riot fan out new Detroit.

Lord, long the day done—lapse, & by bootstraps,
oaths & toads, tranquil microseconds,
memory engulfing, odor of bacon burning
again—phantasmagoria prolix—

a rapture, though, of the Kingdom here here now
in the heart of a child—not far, nor hard to come by,
but natural as water falling, cupped
& lapped & slaking the child's dusty thirst!

If He for me as I feel for my daughter,
being His son, I'll sweat no more tonight
but happy hymn & sleep. I have got it made,
and so have all we of contrition, for

if He loves me He must love everybody
and Origen was right & Hell is empty
or will be at apocatastasis.
Sinners, sin on. We'll suffer now & later

but not forever, dear friends & brothers! Moreover:
my old Black freshman friend's mild formula
for the quarter-mile, 'I run the first 220
as fast as possible, to get out in front.

Then I run the second 220 even faster,
to stay out in front.' So may I run for You,
less laggard lately, less deluded man
of oxblood expectation
with fiery little resiny aftertastes.

Heard sapphire flutings. The winter will end. I remember You.
The sky was red. My pillow's cold & blanched.
There are no fair bells in this city. This fireless house
lies down at Your disposal as usual! Amen!

II

Washington in Love

I
Rectitude, and the terrible upstanding member

II
The music of our musketry is: *beautiful*

III
Intolerable Sally, loved in vain

IV
Mr Adams of Massachusetts . . . I accept, gentlemen.

V
Aloes. Adders. Roman gratitude.

VI
My porch elevation from the Potomac is 174′, 7½″.

VII
Bring the wounded, Martha! *Bring the wounded, men.*

Beethoven Triumphant

1

Dooms menace from tumults. Who's immune
among our mightier of headed men?
Chary with his loins
womanward, he begot us an enigma.

2

Often pretended he was absentminded
whenas he couldn't hear; and often was.
'. . . always *he*, he everywhere, as one says of Napoleon'
(Sir John Russell in '21 hearing a Trio)

3

O migratory rooms, the unworthy brothers, the worthless
nephew!
One time his landlord tipped a hat to him;
Beethoven moved. Awkward & plangent
charged to the Archduke's foot,—who told his court 'Leave him
alone.'

4

My unpretending love's the B flat major
by the old Budapest done. Schnabel did record
the Diabelli varia. I can't get a copy.
Then there's Casals I have, 101, both parts.

5

Moments are, early on in the 4th Piano Concerto
show him at his unrivalled middle best.

It does go up and up, and down lingeringly.
Miser & Timon-giving, by queer turns.

6

They wanted him London, partout. 'Too late,' 'Too late'
he muttered, and mimicked piano-playing.
Prodigious, so he never knew his age
his father'd lied about.

7

Whatever his kindness to Rossini and contempt for Italians,
if down he sat a while in an exquisite chair
it had to be thrown out (five witnesses,
none of whom says quite why).

8

O did he sleep sound? Heavy, heavy that.
Waked at 3:30 not by some sonata
but by a botched rehearsal of the Eighth
where all thing has to go right

(Koussevitzky will make it, Master; lie back down)

9

Lies of his fluency from Betty von Arnim
to eager Goethe, who'd not met the man.
Fact is, he stumbled at the start
and in the sequence, stumbled in the middle,

10

Often unsure at the end—shown by his wilderness
on-sketchings encrusted like Tolstoy (not Mozart:
who'd, ripping napkins, the whole strict in mind
before notes serried; limitationless, unlike you).

au moins à Joséphine? save the world-famous unsent
or when retrieved and past-death-treasured letter?

20

Deception spared. No doubt he took one look:
'Not mine; I can't make a kroner there.'
Straightforward staves, dark bars,
late motions toward the illegible. Musical thighs,

21

spared deep age. Out at prime, in a storm
inaudible thunder he went, upon his height.
The other day I called our chief prose-writer
at home a thousand miles off and began
'How are you, Sir?'   out of three decades' amity

22

'I'm OLD,' he said. Neither of us laughed.
Spared deep age, Beethoven. I wish you'd caught
young Schubert's last chamberworks and the *Winterreise*
you could have read through, puffing.

23

Ah but the indignities you flew free from,
your self-abasements even would increase
together with your temper, evil already,
'some person of bad character, churlish & eccentric'
For refusing to scribble a word of introduction:
'He is an unlicked bear'—almost Sam Johnson.

24

An entertainer, a Molière, in the onset
under too nearly Mozart's aegis,
the mysteries of Oedipus old were not beyond you.
Islands of suffering & disenchantment & enchantment.

It does go up and up, and down lingeringly.
Miser & Timon-giving, by queer turns.

6

They wanted him London, partout. 'Too late,' 'Too late'
he muttered, and mimicked piano-playing.
Prodigious, so he never knew his age
his father'd lied about.

7

Whatever his kindness to Rossini and contempt for Italians,
if down he sat a while in an exquisite chair
it had to be thrown out (five witnesses,
none of whom says quite why).

8

O did he sleep sound? Heavy, heavy that.
Waked at 3:30 not by some sonata
but by a botched rehearsal of the Eighth
where all thing has to go right

(Koussevitzky will make it, Master; lie back down)

9

Lies of his fluency from Betty von Arnim
to eager Goethe, who'd not met the man.
Fact is, he stumbled at the start
and in the sequence, stumbled in the middle,

10

Often unsure at the end—shown by his wilderness
on-sketchings encrusted like Tolstoy (not Mozart:
who'd, ripping napkins, the whole strict in mind
before notes serried; limitationless, unlike you).

11
Inundations out from ground zero.
Back from an over-wealth, the simplification of Necessity.
When brother Johann signed 'Real Estate Owner,' you: 'Brain
                                                        owner.'
And what, among fumbling notes, in the nights, did you read?

12
Coffee and tallow spot your *Odyssey*
though, and when Schindler was an arse to ask
your drift in Opus 31 and the Appassionata
you uttered at him, cheerful, 'Just read *The Tempest.*'

13
Thinking presides, some think now,—only presides—
at the debate of the Instincts; but presides,
over powers, over love, hurt-back.
You grumbled: 'Religion and Figured Bass are closed concepts.
Don't argue.'

14
To disabuse the 'Heiligerdankgesang'?
Men up to now sometimes weep openly.
Tortured your surly star to sing impossibly
against the whole (small) thwarting orchestra.
One chord thrusts, as it must

15
find allies, foes, resolve, in subdued crescendo.
Unfazed, you built-in the improbable.
You clowned. You made throats swallow
and shivered the backs of necks.
You made quiver with glee, at will; not long.
This world is of male energy male pain.

16

Softnesses, also yours, which become us.
What stayed your chosen instrument? The 'cello?
At two points. At others, the forte-piano.
At others, the fiddles & viola & 'cello.

17

I'm hard to you, odd nights. I bulge my brain,
my shut chest already suffers,—so I play blues
and Haydn whom you—both the which touch but they don't
                                        ache me.
I'm less inured in your disaster corner,
Master. You interfere.
                    O yes we interfere
or we're mere sweetening: what? the alkali lives
around and after ours. Sleeking down nerves
Passing time dreaming. And you did do that   too.
       There hover Things cannot be banned by you;
damned few.
                    If we take our head in our ears and listen
Ears! Ears! the Devil paddled in you

18

heard not a hill flute or a shepherd sing!
tensing your vision onto an alarm
of gravid measures, sequent to demure,
all we fall, absently foreknowing. .
You force a blurt: Who was I?
Am I these tutti, am I this rallentando?
This entrance of the oboe?
                    I am all these
the sane man makes reply on the locked ward.

19

Did ever you more than (clearly) cope odd women?
save clumsy uncommitted overtures

au moins à Joséphine? save the world-famous unsent
or when retrieved and past-death-treasured letter?

20

Deception spared. No doubt he took one look:
'Not mine; I can't make a kroner there.'
Straightforward staves, dark bars,
late motions toward the illegible. Musical thighs,

21

spared deep age. Out at prime, in a storm
inaudible thunder he went, upon his height.
The other day I called our chief prose-writer
at home a thousand miles off and began
'How are you, Sir?'   out of three decades' amity

22

'I'm OLD,' he said. Neither of us laughed.
Spared deep age, Beethoven. I wish you'd caught
young Schubert's last chamberworks and the *Winterreise*
you could have read through, puffing.

23

Ah but the indignities you flew free from,
your self-abasements even would increase
together with your temper, evil already,
'some person of bad character, churlish & eccentric'
For refusing to scribble a word of introduction:
'He is an unlicked bear'—almost Sam Johnson.

24

An entertainer, a Molière, in the onset
under too nearly Mozart's aegis,
the mysteries of Oedipus old were not beyond you.
Islands of suffering & disenchantment & enchantment.

25

But the brother charged the dying brother board & lodging.
Bedbugs biting, stench, unquenchable thirst,
ungovernable swelling. Then the great Malfatti
gave up on, and accorded frozen punch ad lib.

26

Your body-filth flowed on to the middle of the floor
'I shall, no doubt, soon be going above'
sweat beading you, gasping of Shakespeare,
knocking over the picture of Haydn's birthplace.

27

They said you died.   '20,000 persons of every class
clashed at the gates of the house of mourning, till they locked
                                                           then

Franz Schubert stalked the five hundred feet to the church.
It's a lie! You're all over my wall!

You march and chant around here! I hear your thighs.

Your Birthday in Wisconsin You Are 140

'One of the wits of the school' your chum would say—
Hot diggity!—   What the *hell* went wrong for you,
Miss Emily,—besides the 'pure & terrible' Congressman
your paralyzing papa,—and Mr Humphrey's dying
          & Benjamin's the other reader? . . .

Fantastic at 32 outpour, uproar, 'terror
since September, I could tell to none'
after your 'Master' moved his family West
and timidly to Mr Higginson:
          'say if my verse is alive.'

Now you wore only white, now you did not appear,
till frantic 50 when you hurled your heart
down before Otis, who would none of it
thro' five years for 'Squire Dickinson's cracked daughter'
          awful by months, by hours . . .

Well. Thursday afternoon, I'm in W———
drinking your ditties, and (dear) *they* are *alive*,—
more so than (bless her) Mrs F who teaches
farmers' red daughters & their beaux *my* ditties
          and yours & yours & yours!
          Hot diggity!

Drugs Alcohol Little Sister

(1887–1914)

WHEN I peered out, he had nine nights to spare
after his gun was man-handled from him
while the dying in his care
mountained and the weakened mind gave way.

So far off to my flatland flew no moan
who'd fail to focus yet for silly weeks.
I shoot him, though, a fellow agony
then I could hardly coo now I must speak

(back from this *schwartze Verwesung* whose white arms
lean subtle over ivories & blacks
and I am sweating, her blind scent subdues
ordure & the hiss of souls escaping)

for let us not all together in such pain
dumb apart pale into oblivion—no!
Trakl, con the male nurse.
Surmounted by carrion, cry out   and overdose & go.

In Memoriam (1914-1953)

I

Took my leave (last) five times before the end
and even past these precautions lost the end.
Oh, I *was* highlone in the corridor
        fifteen feet from his bed

where no other hovered, nurse or staff or friend,
and only the terrible breathing ever took place,
but trembling nearer after some small time
        I came on the tent collapsed

and silence—O unable to say when.
I stopped panicked a nurse, she a doctor
in twenty seconds, he pulled the plasticine,
        bent over, and shook his head at me.

Tubes all over, useless versus coma,
on the third day his principal physician
told me to pray he'd die, brain damage such.
        His bare stub feet stuck out.

II

So much for the age's prodigy, born one day
before I surfaced—when this fact emerged
Dylan grew stuffy and would puff all up
        rearing his head back and roar

'A little more—more—*respect* there, Berryman!'
Ah he had that,—so far ahead of me,
I half-adored him for his intricate booms & indecent tales
       almost entirely untrue.

Scorn bottomless for elders: we were twenty-three
but Yeats I worshipped: he was amused by this,
all day the day set for my tea with the Great Man
       he plotted to turn me up drunk.

Downing me daily at shove-ha'penny
with *English* on the thing. C——— would slump there
plump as a lump for hours, my word how that changed!
       Hard on her widowhood—

     III
Apart a dozen years, sober in Seattle
'After many a summer' he intoned
putting out a fat hand. We shook hands.
       How very shook to see him.

His talk, one told me, clung latterly to Eden,
again & again of the Garden & the Garden's flowers,
not ever the Creator, only of that creation
       with a radiant will to go there.

I have sat hard for twenty years on this
mid potpals' yapping, and O I sit still still
though I quit crying that same afternoon
       of the winter of his going.

Scribbled me once, it's around somewhere or other,
word of their 'Edna Millay cottage' at Laugharne

saying come down to and disarm a while
    and down a many few.

O down a many few, old friend,
and down a many few.

III

Gislebertus' Eve

*Most men are not wicked . . . They
are sleep-walkers, not evildoers.*
KAFKA TO G JANOUCH

Eve & her envy roving slammed me down
prone in discrepancy: I can't get things right:
the passion for secrets the passion worst of all,
the ultimate human, from Leonardo & Darwin

to the austere Viennese with the cigar
and Bohr a-musing: 'The opposite of a true
statement is a false statement. But the opposite
of a profound truth may be another profound truth.'

So now we see where we are, which is all-over
we're nowhere, son, and suffering we know it,
rapt in delusion, where weird particles
frantic & Ditheletic orbit our

revolutionary natures. She snaked out a soft
small willing hand, curved her ivory fingers on
a new taste sensation, in reverie over
something other,
sank her teeth in, and offered him a bite.

I too find it delicious.

Scholars at the Orchid Pavilion

1

Sozzled, Mo-tsu, after a silence, vouchsafed
a word alarming: 'We must love them all!'
Affronted, the fathers jumped.
'Yes' he went madly on and waved in quest
of his own dreadful subject 'O the fathers'
he cried 'must not be all!'
Whereat upon consent we broke up for the day.

2

The bamboo's bending power formed our theme
next dawn, under a splendid wind. The water
flapped to our tender gaze.
Girls came & crouched with tea. Great Wu pinched one,
forgetting his later nature. How the wind howled,
tranquil was our pavilion,
watching & reflecting, fingering bamboo.

3

'Wild geese & bamboo' muttered Ch'en Hung-shou
'block out our boundaries of fearful wind.
Neither requires shelter.
I shelter among painters, doing bamboo.
The young shoots unaffected by the wind
mock our love for their elders.'
Mo-tsu opened his mouth & closed it to again.

4

'The bamboo of the Ten Halls' went on Ch'en
'of my time, are excellently made.
I cannot find so well
ensorcelled those of later or former time.
Let us apply the highest praise, pure wind,
to those surpassing masters;—
having done things, a thing, along that line myself.'

Tampa Stomp

THE first signs of the death of the boom came in the summer,
early, and everything went like snow in the sun.
Out of their office windows. There was miasma,
a weight beyond enduring, the city reeked of failure.

The eerie, faraway scream of a Florida panther,
gu-roomp of a bull-frog. One broker we knew
drunk-driving down from Tarpon Springs flew free
when it spiralled over & was dead without one mark on him.

The Lord fled that forlorn peninsula
of fine sunlight and millions of fishes & moccasins
& Spanish moss & the Cuban bit my father
bedded & would abandon Mother for.

Ah, an antiquity, a chatter of ghosts.
Half the fish now in half the time
since those blue days died. We're running out
of time & fathers, sore, artless about it.

Old Man Goes South Again Alone

O PARAKEETS & avocets, O immortelles
& ibis, scarlet under that stunning sun,
deliciously & tired I come
toward you in orbit, Trinidad!—albeit without the one

I would bring with me to those isles & seas,
leaving her airborne westward thro' great snows
whilst I lapse on your beaches
sandy with dancing, dark   moist eyes among my toes.

The Handshake, The Entrance

'You've got to cross that lonesome valley' and
'You've got to cross it by yourself.'
Ain't no one gwine cross it for you,
You've got to cross it by yourself.
Some say John was a baptist, some say John was a Jew,
some say John was just a natural man

addin' he's a preacher too?

'You've got to cross that lonesome valley,'
Friends & lovers, link you and depart.
This one is strictly for me.
I shod myself & said goodbye to Sally
Murmurs of other farewells half broke my heart
I set out sore indeed.

The High King failed to blossom on my enterprise.
Solely the wonderful sun shone down like lead.
Through the ridges I endured,
down in no simple valley I opened my eyes,
with my strong walk down in the vales & dealt with death.
I increased my stride, cured.

38

Lines to Mr Frost

F<small>ELLED</small> in my tracks by your tremendous horse
slain in its tracks by the angel of good God,
I wonder toward your marvellous tall art
warning away maybe in that same morning

you squandered afternoon of your great age
on my good gravid wife & me, with tales
gay of your cunning & colossal fame
& awful character, and—Christ—I see

I know & can do nothing, and don't mind—
you're talking about American power and how
somehow we've got to be got to give it up—
so help me, in my poverty-stricken way

I said the same goddamn thing yesterday
to my thirty kids, so I was almost ready
to hear you from the grave with these passionate grave
last words, and frankly Sir you fill me with joy.

He Resigns

AGE, and the deaths, and the ghosts.
Her having gone away
in spirit from me. Hosts
of regrets come & find me empty.

I don't feel this will change.
I don't want any thing
or person, familiar or strange.
I don't think I will sing

any more just now;
or ever. I must start
to sit with a blind brow
above an empty heart.

No

SHE says: *Seek help!* Ha-ha Ha-ha & Christ.
Gall in every direction, putrid olives,
stench of the Jersey flats, the greasy clasp
crones in black doorways afford their violent clients

A physicist's lovely wife grinned to me in Cambridge
she only liked, apart from getting gamblers hot
& stalk out on them, a wino for the night
in a room off Scollay Square, a bottle, his efforts

Dust in my sore mouth, this deafening wind,
frightful spaces down from all sides, I'm pale
I faint for some soft & solid & sudden way out
as quiet as hemlock in that Attic prose

with comprehending friends attending—
a certain reluctance but desire here too,
the sweet cold numbing upward from my burning feet,
a last & calm request, which will be granted.

The Form

Mutinous and free I drifted off
unsightly. I did not see the creatures watch.
I had forgotten about the creatures, which
were kind, and whether any of them was mine.

I am a daemon. Ah, when Mother was ill
a Sister took me into their little chapel
to admire the plaster angels: 'Mine are real,'
I said, 'and fly around the chapel on my farm.'

O torso hurled high in great 'planes from town
down on confulsing town, brainsick applause
thick to sick ear, through sixteen panicked nights
a trail of tilted bottles. I had no gun,

and neither Wednesday nor Thursday did buy one
but Friday and I put it in my bag
and bought a wide-eyed and high-yaller whore
for company of darkness. Deep in dream

I saw myself upreared like William the Silent
over his tomb in Delft, armoured and impotent;
she shook me screaming. In another place
I shuddered as I combed and saw my face.

Swallowing, I felt myself deranged
and would be ever so. He has spewed me out.
I wandered, for some reason, raging, home
where then I really hurt. All that life ahead alone

vised me from midnight. I prepared for dawn.
An odd slight thought like a key slid somewhere:
'Only tomorrow.' Wondering, I said: 'Oh.
It's possible, then.'
       My light terrible body unlocked, I leaned upon You.

Ecce Homo

Long long with wonder I thought you human,
almost beyond humanity but not.
Once, years ago, only in a high bare hall
of the great Catalan museum over Barcelona,
   I thought you might be more—

a Pantocrator glares down, from San Clemente de Tahull,
making me feel you probably were divine,
but not human, through that majestic image.
Now I've come on something where you seem both—
   a photograph of it only—

Burgundian, of painted & gilt wood,
life-size almost (not that we know your Semitic stature),
attenuated, your dead head bent forward sideways,
your long feet hanging, your thin long arms out
   in unconquerable beseeching—

A Prayer After All

F<small>ATHER</small>, Father, I am overwhelmed.
I cannot speak tonight.
Do you receive me back into Your sight?
It seems it must be so, for

strangely the Virgin came into my mind
as I stood beside my bed—
whom I not only have not worshipped
since childhood, but also

harsh words have said of, that she pushed her Son
before his time was come
which he rebuked her for, and leaving home
repudiated hers & her—

and for no reason, standing in the dark
before I had knelt down
(as is my custom) to speak with You, I found
my tongue feeling its way

thro' the Hail Mary, trying phrase by phrase
its strangeness, for the unwelcome
to my far mind estranged, awaiting some
unacceptable sense, and

Father I was amazed I could find none
and I have walked downstairs

to sit & wonder: You must have been Theirs
all these years, and They Yours,

and now I suppose I have prayed to You after all
and Her and I suppose she is the Queen of Heaven
under Your greater glory, even
more incomprehensible but forgiving glory.

Back

I was out of your Church for 43 years, my Dear;
adopted back in, welling blood.
Admire the techniques of your ministers
I must, succeeding, but could not enjoy them

during the rite: for the man in fury,
possessed by his own tumultuous & burning energy,
to bring to a halt is hard as tungsten carbide
and crook his knees is harder than to die.

Exceptional, singular, & mysterious,
ochered, forbidden to utter,
the revolted novice & veteran thro' cold night
vigilant in the forest, a caring beast,

becoming sacral, perforates his nose
at first glow, in honour of the Mother.
Whose coming to be is constant,
Thou hast caused her coming-to-be in beauty.

Hel*lo*

H el*lo* there, Biscuit! You're a better-looking broad
by much than, and your sister's dancing up & down.
'I just gave one mighty Push'
your mother says, and we are all in business.

I thought your mother might powder my knuckles
gript at one point, with wild eyes on my tie
'Don't move!' and then the screams began,
they wheeled her off, and we are all in business.

I wish I knew what business (son) we're in
I can't wait seven weeks to see her grin
I'm not myself, we are all changing here
direction *and* velocity, to   accommodate you, dear.

IV SCHERZO

Navajo Setting the Record Straight

'Warrior Who Went With a Crowd, my sand-painter
                                    grandfather,'
said Axel no-middle-initial Mankey Jr
to the Marine sarge, 'served at Fort Wingate
as a sergeant-major scout, and he was buried

with full military honors in Arlington.
So screw you, Sergeant, *and* your Greek accent.
Moreover, from the black world into the blue
came The First People, to the yellow world,

and finally into the present sick white world
thro' a giant reed,—which may be seen to this day
near Silverton, Colorado. Yah-ah-teh.'
His unbound black locks wind-flared as back at Left & Right
                                    Mittens
motherless next to the earth-covered log hogan of Mrs Hetty
                                    Rye.

Henry by Night

HENRY's nocturnal habits were the terror of his women.
First it appears he snored, lying on his back.
Then he thrashed & tossed,
changing position like a task fleet. Then, inhuman,
he woke every hour or so—they couldn't keep track
of mobile Henry, lost

at 3 a.m., off for more drugs or a cigarette,
reading old mail, writing new letters, scribbling
excessive Songs;
back then to bed, to the old tune or get set
for a stercoraceous cough, without quibbling
death-like. His women's wrongs

they hoarded & forgave, mysterious, sweet;
but you'll admit it was no way to live
or even keep alive.
I won't mention the dreams I won't repeat
sweating & shaking: something's gotta give:
up for good at five.

Henry's Understanding

He was reading late, at Richard's, down in Maine,
aged 32? Richard & Helen long in bed,
my good wife long in bed.
All I had to do was strip & get into my bed,
putting the marker in the book, & sleep,
& wake to a hot breakfast.

Off the coast was an island, P'tit Manaan,
the bluff from Richard's lawn was almost sheer.
A chill at four o'clock.
It only takes a few minutes to make a man.
A concentration upon now & here.
Suddenly, unlike Bach,

& horribly, unlike Bach, it occurred to me
that *one* night, instead of warm pajamas,
I'd take off all my clothes
& cross the damp cold lawn & down the bluff
into the terrible water & walk forever
under it out toward the island.

Defensio in Extremis

I said: Mighty men have encamped against me,
and they have questioned not only the skill of my defences
but my sincerity.
Now, Father, let them have it.

Thou knowest, whatever their outcry & roar,
in quietness I read my newly simple heart
after so far returning.
O even X, great Y, fine Z

splinter at my procedures and my ends.
Surely their spiritual life is not what it might be?
Surely they are half-full of it?
Tell them to leave me damned well alone with my insights.

Damn You, Jim D., You Woke Me Up

I THOUGHT I'd say a thing to please myself
& why not him, about his talent, to him
or to some friend who'd maybe pass it on
because he printed a sweet thing about me
a long long time ago, & because of gladness
to see a good guy *get out* of the advertising racket
& suddenly make like the Great Chicago Fire—
yes that was it, fine, fine—(this was a dream
woke me just now)—I'll get a pen & paper
at once & put that down, I thought, and I went
away from where I was, up left thro' a garden
in the direction of the Avenue
but got caught on a smart kid's escalator
going uphill against it, got entangled,
a girl was right behind me in the dark,
they hoisted up some cart and we climbed on
& over the top & *down*, thinking Jesus
I'll break my arse but a parked car broke the fall
I landed softly there in the dark street
having forgotten all about   the Great Chicago Fire!

V

Somber Prayer

O MY Lord, I am not eloquent
neither heretofore, nor since Thou hast spoken . . .
but I am slow of speech, of a dim tongue.
He mentions, here, Thy 'counsel and dominion';

so I will borrow Newton's mouth. Spare me
Uccello's ark-locked lurid deluge, I'm
the brutal oaf from the barrel stuck mid-scene,—
or ghost me past the waters . . . Miriam . . .

A twelve-year-old all solemn, sorry-faced,
described himself lately as 'a lifetime prick.'
Me too. Maladaptive devices.
At fifty-five half-famous & effective, I still feel rotten about
myself.

Panicky weekdays, I pray hard,
not worthy.
Sucking, clinging, following, crying, smiling,
I come Your child to You.

Unknowable? perhaps not altogether

I DARE interpret: Adonai of rescue.
Whatever and ever other I have lain skew over
however O little else around You know
I doubt I'm wrong on this.
Augustine and Pascal swore the same strange.

Yet young men young men in the paddies rescue.

Add Sway omnicompetent, add pergalactic Intellect,
forbearance invisible, a tumbling thunder of laughter
(or whence our so alert pizzazz & laughter?),
an imagination of the queens of Chartres the kings there, if
                                          these only, still
we're trans-acting with You.

Minnesota Thanksgiving

For that free Grace bringing us past terrible risks
& thro' great griefs surviving to this feast
sober & still, with the children unborn and born,
among brave friends, Lord, we stand again in debt
and find ourselves in the glad position: Gratitude.

We praise our ancestors who delivered us here
within warm walls all safe, aware of music,
likely toward ample & attractive meat
with whatever accompaniment
Kate in her kind ingenuity has seen fit to devise,

and we hope—across the most strange year to come—
continually to do them and You not sufficient honour
but such as we become able to devise
out of a decent or joyful *conscience* & thanksgiving.
Yippee!
          Bless then, as Thou wilt, this wilderness board.

A Usual Prayer

ACCORDING to Thy will: That this day only
I may avoid the vile
and baritone away in a broader chorus
of to each other decent forbearance & even aid.

Merely sensational let's have today,
lacking mostly thinking,—
men's thinking being eighteen-tenths deluded.
Did I get this figure out of St Isaac of Syria?

For fun: find me among   my self-indulgent artbooks
a new drawing by Ingres!
For discipline, two self-denying minus-strokes
and my wonted isometrics, barbells, & antiphons.

Lord of happenings, & little things,
muster me westward fitter to my end—
which has got to be Your strange end for me—
and toughen me effective to the tribes en route.

Overseas Prayer

Good evening. At the feet of the king, my Lord,
I fall seven & yet seven times.
Behold what insult has Your servant suffered
from Shuwardata and Milkiln & his ilk.

Put them under saws, & under harrows of iron,
& under axes of iron, make them pass thro' the brick-kiln
lest at any time they flirt at me again.
Enjoin them to the blurred & breathless dead.

The Valley of the Cheesemakers has disappeared
also, my Lord. Your precincts are in ruin,
your revenues ungathered. Minarets
blot our horizon as I pen, my Lord.

I feel myself a deep & old objection.
You gave me not a very able father,
joyless at last, Lord, and sometimes I hardly
(thinking on him) perform my duty to you.

Ah then I mutter 'Forty-odd years past.
Do I yet repine?' and go about your business,—
a fair wind and the honey lights of home
being all I ask this wind-torn foreign evening.

Amos

For three insane things evil, and for four,
will I vex Pekin in the latter days,
their ancestors shall suffer for their children
in turbid horror: so saith the Lord.

For three insane things evil, and for four,
grieve will I Kremlin presently, & the Urals,
& Omsk, and I will tear their leaderhood
that many may fly home: saith the Lord.

For three insane things evil, and for four,
torment will I the North & South & East
& West with understanding, where they stand,
and I will unman & de-parent them
and will deprive them: thus saith the Lord.

Certainty Before Lunch

Ninety percent of the mass of the Universe
(90%!) may be gone in collapsars,
pulseless, lightless, forever, if they exist.
My friends the probability man & I

& his wife the lawyer are taking a country walk
in the flowerless April snow in exactly two hours
and maybe won't be back. Finite & unbounded
the massive spirals absolutely fly

distinctly apart, by math *and* observation,
current math, this morning's telescopes
& inference. My wife is six months gone
so won't be coming. That mass must be somewhere!

or not? just barely possibly *may not*
BE anywhere? My Lord, I'm glad we don't
on x or y depend for Your being there.
I know You are there. The sweat is, I am here.

The Prayer of the Middle-Aged Man

AMID the doctors in the Temple at twelve, between
mother & host at Cana implored too soon,
in the middle of disciples, the midst of the mob,
between the High Priest and the Procurator,
     among the occupiers,

between the malefactors, and 'stetit in medio,
et dixit, Pax vobis' and 'ascensit ad mediam
Personarum et caelorum,' dear my Lord,
mercy a sinner nailed dead-centre too,
     pray not implored too late,—

for also Ezra stood between the seven & the six,
     restoring the new Law.

'How Do You Do, Dr Berryman, Sir?'

EDGY, perhaps. *Not* on the point of bursting-forth,
but toward that latitude,—I think? *Not* 'shout loud & march
straight.'
Each lacks something in some direction. I
am not entirely at the mercy of.

The tearing of hair no.

Pickt up pre-dawn & tortured and detained,
Mr Tan Mam and many other students
sit tight but vocal in illegal cells
and as for Henry Pussycat   he'd just as soon be dead

(on the Promise of—I know it sounds incredible—
if can he muster penitence enough—
he can't though—
glory)

The Facts & Issues

I REALLY believe He's here all over this room
in a motor hotel in Wallace Stevens' town.
I admit it's weird; and *could*—or could it?—not be so;
but frankly I don't think there's a molecular chance of that.
It doesn't seem hypothesis. Thank heavens
millions agree with me, or mostly do,
and have done ages of our human time,
among whom were & still are some very sharp cookies.
I don't exactly feel missionary about it,
though it's *very* true I wonder if I should.
I regard the boys who don't buy this as deluded.
Of course they regard me no doubt as deluded.
Okay with me! And not the hell with them
at *all*—no!—I feel *dubious* on Hell—
it's here, all right, but elsewhere, after? Screw that,
I feel pretty sure that evil simply ends
for the doer (having wiped him out,
by the way, usually) where good goes on,
or good *may* drop dead too: I don't think so:
I can't say I have hopes in that department
myself, I lack ambition just just there,
I know that Presence says it's mild, and it's mild,
but being what I am I wouldn't care
to dare go nearer. Happy to be here
and to have been here, with such lovely ones
so infinitely better, but to me
even in their suffering infinitely kind
& blessing. I am a greedy man, of course,
but I wouldn't want that kind of luck continued,—